A'holes That I've Known

by Bill Rosoman

ISBN 978-1-927157-09-1

Table of Contents

About the Author

I have lived an interesting and varied life. Currently I am unemployed and living on the road in a Mobile Home (RV). Life is full of surprises and chances.

I really regret little in my life, of cause if I had my life over again there are things that I would change. But hey life goes on and follows it's path.

This is our online business card. Just scan with your smart phone or computer to see the card.

I am currently publishing and writing some more ebooks. This is interesting and fun. I am also making some money!
https://www.smashwords.com/profile/view/leftfieldnz

I have worked with technology for many years and have been quite prophetic over the years. I have been working on Books and Ebooks online for many years now. It is starting to pay some dividends and we are starting to get some rewards.

I am a Pacifist at heart but if push comes to shove would defend myself. If my Life was Threatened the I Would Act.

I have only been really threatened four times in my life. These are outlined in this book.

I consider myself an Optimistic Realist.

"Optimism has a Chance
Persimmon has no Chance.

Life has had its ups and downs, but general my life has been and is great.

My glass is always half full.

I try and treat all people with respect. But being nice and friendly is a two way street. So if people are nice to me I am nice to them.

If they wish to be mean and nasty, either I walk away or they get what they give!

I am not bitter and twisted, angry or full of hate. Merely a student of human nature.

I do not hate anybody as I do not have the time or energy as life is too short to be side tracked by negative BS.

Life is a Bitch
And then you Marry One
LOL

The list of A'holes is in some sort of order with the biggest A'holes at the .

Mind you some are not so much A'holes but funny, misguided etc.

Being confident, articulate and assertive is the way to go, no door mouse for me. LOL

Arohanui
Bill Rosoman

Disclaimer

I have taken care to not identify people and places too much. I apologise if anyone takes offence. But these events are my true recollection of what happened.

I take no responsibility for any offence taken, this book is not aimed at offending people but pointing out that in life some nice people most of the time and one faces the odd A'hole.

If you discover one of these A'holes is you, well as they say if the cloth fits, wear it!

Some of the A'holes That I've Known

G the Grump

This would be my number one A'hole. And the worlds worst boss.

I worked at a Service Station (Gas Station) on the Night Shift for five years. All I got from G and his wife was grief. Hardly ever did I get praise, a good word or anything positive.

I was accused of this that and everything, most of which was BS. But if I stood up for myself and challenged them I was considered a stirrer and just looking for trouble.

I used to get a pie delivery every morning and had to count them an put them in the fridge. You had to move the old pies forward and put the new pies at the back. I was always accused of not doing this, but in fact it is what I did. Not once was I shown or told what they think I did wrong. This was not helped by two employees who at different times did the shift after mine. It is true it was a important shift as it did the daily totals etc. But for these two the job went to their heads and they went on a power trip and would pot you into the boss for any little thing. The daily delivery of milk was the same story.

However the big hassle was being short in your till. G the grump would always say you had to make up the short fall. He would try and intimidate the younger employees. I was there for five years and it is only in the last few months I was short in my till. G tried to say you have to pay. I said that it was an honest mistake maybe, or perhaps there was an error somewhere else in the system. I also explained that I had probably served 100,000 people and only made a hand full of mistakes. But he would bang on. He would call me into the office and try and give me a grilling. I said I was not going to pay the lousy $20 as I did not do anything wrong and that if he tried to take it out of my pay I would sue him. He scoffed and said were, I said the employment court. He said that this was his business and he had run it his way for 37 years and that law did not apply to him. I said what about the Tax Department, Health and Safety etc. He said no it did not apply to him. He said that's the trouble with you Bill you always want to argue now bugger off. Some much for a fair hearing.

The first time I was short was a real laugh. While G the Grump was having a go at me about being short $20 in my till, his partner was in Dubai on holiday having $300 afternoon teas (as he told me at a Christmas BBQ). G did not get the irony, that it was the employees like me that allowed G and his partner to have expensive holidays several times a year.

When one night I was robbed of money and cigarettes at knife point, G the Grump wanted to give me a written warning but could not on a technicality. I said what about improving the security in a couple of areas, he said no we've spent enough money on that shit!

So much for him caring about staff or their health and safety.

I quit as I was not prepared to be working for this A'hole anymore.

Police hunt robbers in crime wave

By Belinda Feek

Hamilton police are hunting at least two people wanted for up to seven of the unsolved aggravated robberies in the city.

There have been eight aggravated robberies in the Waikato in the past week and about 25 aggravated robberies since May 31.

The latest both happened on Tuesday night.

A man, armed with a knife, stormed into Dinsdale Video Ezy about 9.45pm, making demands before the owner escaped.

Then at midnight, a man, again armed with a knife, walked into the [illegible] demanding cash and cigarettes before driving off in a dark-coloured sedan.

Officer in charge of Hamilton CIB, Detective Senior Sergeant Chris Page, told the Waikato Times yesterday that three of the robberies – at two service stations and Video Ezy – were believed to be linked.

He also revealed police were hunting at least two people, probably more, whom they believe are responsible for up to seven of the current unsolved aggravated robberies.

"We have a series of robberies of which we believe a number of them are committed by at least two, and possibly others, working with that group of two ... the consistent theme is that these guys commit their offences in groups."

So far a group of three, a pair and a group of five people have been arrested.

J the Maniac

I managed a Hotel and Training Venue for awhile. J was the boss. What a devious dude. He could not help himself, he always had to find the angle, how he could manipulate the situation to his advantage.

He threatened me twice.

Once I was at his flat and we discussing something when he jumped and grabbed me with both hands round the throat, I looked up at him and laughed and said “go for it J”.

The second time was when I left. His attitude and deviousness became too much and I decided to quit. He is one of the few people I have ripped off in my life. I took some music CDs and stuff and did a runner, leaving him a note. He rang me saying, “men do not s bullets, and I'm coming after you”. I rang the local Policeman and told him, but nothing came of it.

J is Manic Depressant or Bi-Polar as they call it nowadays.

He at one time sped taking his medication and went crazy for a few days. He was ringing local businesses and trying to do a deal to buy them.

I told his wife she had better do something or I would. Next thing a Police car arrived with two Policemen and a Psychiatrist in the vehicle. One Policeman spoke to me to get the lay of the land. I said J is legally blind but he can see shapes. He is off his tree and has the potential to be violent. The Cop said plan A is we send in the Psychiatrist, plan B is I'll grab the half, you grab the bottom. But he went quietly.

The Hotel was known for it's chilli beef IE the beef was sourced locally and butchered locally which is illegal and hot, hence the chilli beef.

J had lots of other dodges and rackets going as well!

Another racket was his blindness, it was caused in a car accident. He had the hotel that run at a loss for tax purposes of cause. But ACC (Insurance) is based on your previous income. So they had to cook the books over night so he made a profit. He was on $1000 a week. His cost of living like accommodation, food, phone, power, was all on the hotel.

The hotel under his management eventually went belly up.

Mrs A Infant Mistress 1953

Mr and Mrs A were old fashioned school teachers, beat the kids for their own good seemed to be their motto. I guess they were a product of the 1950s and the social norms of the times.

From the day I was five and attended school I was belted on the knuckles with a ruler as I was left handed and that was not allowed. What is a five year old supposed to do! I remember my Dad was told but nothing was done and eventually I became right handed.

On hindsight it did me a favour as it toughened my resolve, it made me ambidextrous and stronger mentally.

It was a tough time, as I was bullied in the play ground as well. Mother took me to school the first day a distance of 2 ½ miles each way and from then on I had to walk to school myself come rain or shine.

The funniest other thing I remember about my young school days was having health checks. I was born with a hernia and was on a waiting list for 12 years as it was non-urgent. They spent all their time feeling my nuts and it was not till I was 18 and went for a drivers licence that I found out I had bad eyesight.

I thought everybody squinted at the blackboard.

Mr A Headmaster circa 1958

One day I followed a Prefect into the grounds of the school riding on my bike as the Prefect was as well. The Prefect then turned round and gave me a detention as it was not permitted. I was sent to the Headmaster Mr A.

He said I am going to strap you on the hand for breaking the rules. I said but the Prefect did it too. He said never mind hold out your hand. I refused, he was most put out and made me stand in the corner of his office. Ever now and then he would ask are you going to hold out my hand and I said no.

About 2pm my Mother was summoned and was crying that I had

brought the family into disrepute and it was a major disaster.

I held out my hand and got a tap from the strap and was told to return to class.

What an A'hole.

K the Junkie

I have known K for most of his life. I said to him when he was in his early teens that you know the difference between right and wrong, and that if you do wrong you go to prison. He said yes.

He had a wonderful childhood on the farm, he could go hunting and fishing, bike riding, sheep shearing, walks etc. It is true his mother left him when he was very young but his father did the best he could for him. He was diagnosed with HDD and was given some physiological help. One night I sat in with the father and a Psychologist, after I said to M, geez I think the Psychologist is mad. He kept trying to blame the father and looking for excuses and scape goats, not solutions.

M got quite desperate and wrote to the Government Ministry of Social Welfare, but they were of no help. M then called them the Department of Social Destruction.

K started taking drugs and still does to this day. He gets pretty bad, here are a couple of stories.

M his father was dying and in the final weeks, K showed a real interest, saying to me he had got to his father and he had changed his will, K hoped to his favour. I said to him how about we wait till your father dies and then we will find out. M died a short while later. His will in fact was made harder. K was going to get an allowance, but the farm would be managed by Trustees.

K did not like that one bit, a few weeks later he showed up at the farm in the early morning and was marched off the farm with a shotgun in his face by the Manager. He was given a trespass order and is not allowed on the farm, which technically he owns.

I was living down the road a way and earlier had some property stolen, I knew straight away it was K. I tackled him about, but he is a pathological liar and can look you in the face and lie threw his teeth. I said to him you can fool some of the people some of the time but you do not fool me and while I am a pacifist at heart in your case I will make and exception and if it is a question or you or me, I will not be the one dead first.

Some time latter he was staying with my neighbour and screwing her daughter who was either under or barely the legal age for sex of sixteen.

I got pissed off with him and rang the Police. I said you have to do something, you have several arrest warrants and I am telling you were he is. The Cop said leave it with me.

A few days later I got a knock on the door at daylight, it was a Policeman, he said you have to come to the neighbours house and identify that K is there. I went and said to the Policeman I am 99% sure K is in there. The Policeman knocked on the door and said it was the Police. They had about several Police and a Police dog surrounding the house. I nudged the young cop beside me and said what are you going to do. He said what, I said the guy has just shot the gap out the back window. I ran out into the street and was told off as they had let the Police dog loose. But I saw the dog grab him up the street and bring him to the ground so they could handcuff him and take him away.

M's brother farmed the farm next door and was loosing a lot of farm machinery and petrol/diesel, so he fitted an alarm (as did M on his farm). The first person the brother caught was his nephew K.

I said to M that the alarm was not much use because if K came after him and assuming M or K triggered the alarm, it would take 20-30 minutes for someone to turn up at the best of times by which time you would have bleed to death anyway!

K has ripped many many people off and including Motor Bike Gangs. He said to me at his fathers funeral, you were right Bill.

He is still a total loose canon on the run from people and the Police.

K the Wanker

K was a co-worker, he was an A'hole and a perfectionist. I am not a perfectionist, I believe in doing a good job but not to the point of wasting too much time.

The first time K had a go at me was when I was OIC (Officer in Charge). K at the time was courting his what was to be his 3rd wife. He used to take a mattress in his van and go bush with her!

He would then ring up late in the afternoon and have some lame excuse as to were he had been, and then have to work several hours overtime to fix telephones he should have done during the day. A complete rip off.

I gave him a written instruction that he should first ring me before doing any overtime. He took exception and wrote to the bosses.

I found out he had written a letter and read it from the carbon paper he had used. I told the bosses I was being reasonable and they were being gust-less in not standing up to K. I got it in the neck.

The second time K had a go at me was when we were upgrading the telephones in a street by putting the cables underground.

I was the Senior Foreman and said to K, we have finished this house can you go and shift the telephone inside the house.

Two hours later, I still had not seen K, I went to the house and said to K, what the hell are you doing. He said he was trying to do a perfect job, I said you have wasted two hours and the job is as good as it gets.

I returned outside the house and carried on. When K came out of the house he grabbed a shovel and threatened me with it. I said to him that is the second and last time you will threaten me. Next time I go to the Police on an assault charge. At that time I also purchased a .22 rifle, supposedly for Possum hunting but in fact for self-defence.

I told my wife that if K showed up at the door, duck because I would probably shoot him.

I used to help K if he got stuck. The boys used to say why do you help him when you know he hates you. I said I do it for the customer not him.

The classic of that was when our last telephone exchange went from a manual system to an electronic exchange. K was supposed to connect and test what I believe was the last Lotto Terminal to be connected in the whole of New Zealand. It was at the local grocery store.

He rang me and I went done and had a look, I rang the head office and spoke to someone. I lifted the Lotto Machine lid, flickered a couple of switches and we were away. And according K I was the A'hole!

The Vicar circa 1959

I was christened a C of E (Church of England) or Anglican, I did manage to dodge being Confirmed as a Teenager. Not sure whether I was Baptised.

It is not the Vicar per se was an A'hole, but the Church sure are.

I was 11 in 1959.

I was forced to attend Sunday School, but when one Sunday I argued with the young Sunday School Teacher I was stood in the corner.

I used to sit in church and listen to these daft sermons and look around and see particularly the local businessmen, who seemed to be at church to get forgiveness for all there sins committed during the week ripping people off. How hypercritical.

My mother used to send an envelope with the tithe in it, I thought what the hell and used to open it and take half for lollies on the way home.

Religion sucks and so do Vicars! I have seen the light, God is the biggest A'hole I have been forced to think that he is a white middle class male, sitting up there telling me when I can suck eggs, yer right. Get a Life!

Accountant for NR

I was involved in helping some local groups deliver adult education for unemployed people using Government funding.

The money had to be accounted for to several Government Departments and other Stack Holders. The accounts had to pass an annual audit.

One year NRs accounts were lost when the Accountants allowed one of their employees to take them home. He then had a mental breakdown and the accounts could not be found.

I had several meetings with the Accountants and asked them were are the accounts and what were they going to do about it. All they did was stone wall us.

I asked them if they had a Quality Management System They said yes, I asked to see there QMS Documentation, they said no.

I got frustrated and went to the Local Secretary of the Accountants Society. It was obvious that he had been forewarned (it's only a small town). I asked him what he would do and what was the Societies policies on this situation. He said it was none of my business, I asked why, he said because you are member of the public. I could not believe it.

I then rang the National Office of the Accountants Society and got a person who used to live in the town we are talking about. He was horrified and I had the information the next day in the mail.

But locally they just stone walled till we got sick of it. No resolution, no responsibility, no compensation.

These were Professional A'holes.

Lawyer for MT

I was a Trustee of MT for fourteen years. The Trust grew to be quite big. It came to a time were we wanted to change the Trust Deed. A Local Small Town Lawyer told us we would have to go to the High Court to get the changes made.

I heard on the radio a big city Lawyer saying there was a much easier and cheaper way. I rang him and got the information.

I told the Trust what I had done and got told off. However my advice was taken and was correct. We filed the Trust Deed changes and a cheque for a few hundred dollars and the job was done.

I then tried to get to see the Local Secretary of the Law Society, I went to his office but he said he could not see me anytime soon.

That night I was staying with a friend, who as well known in the community. I was knocked over when the Lawyer I had spent time trying to see spoke to my friend for an hour that evening.

I told my friend what I had been doing, and said how come he will not talk to a commoner like me but he can talk for an hour to a local farmer.

What an A'hole!

Nurse H

Nurse H was a wonderful nurse. I have put this because it is quite funny!

I was in a small remote hospital in the 1970s having some haemorrhoids removed.

After my operation I was in a general ward. At night the nurse would come round with a plate full of pills. I am a sensitive soul when it comes to medication (as I have not taken much in my life), I asked what the pills were.

I was told the large pink was a sleeping pill, I said I am not having that, another was anti-biotic, I said that's OK, the rest I can not remember. I think they tried to give every patient a sleeping pill (probably about 20-30 patients) so the nurses got a good nights sleep.

When it came to removing the wad from my rear end, H said I have to have a pain killer Pethidine, I said no as it makes me see double for days. We argued for a good few minutes till H said OK.

She removed the wad and then said, you did not yell, I said because it did not hurt.

Inland Revenue F re MT

I in the 1980s used to run 12 week Computer Training courses in a small rural town, they were also about empowering people. All the students were local unemployed people.

The courses ran for several years. We ran them under a Trust that was in the next big town.

It was at a time when the Inland Revenue Department was installing a $240 million computer system. I was a tutor and the administrator.

We filed all the correct tax returns on a monthly and some on an annual basis.

At sometime the IRD wrote to the course and claimed that the course owed $3000 in unpaid taxes. I was astounded, but thinking about it I figured they had not realised that some taxes like PAYE and GST we paid direct to IRD and some like the annual accounts were done through our parent body.

So I wrote to IRD and pointed this out but got an abrupt reply saying pay up.

Me being me I had good records so I did some research and wrote another letter to IRD explaining that they are mistaken and perhaps because of the new computer system they may have lost the link of our accounts to our parent body. I also asked them to reply to eleven specific points.

They wrote back ignoring my letter and threatening to sue.

At that time there was a good local office in the city, so I went and saw their public advocate. I explained what I had done and the letters. He said what do you want and I said, I want that A'hole F's head on a platter and if IRD take me to court I will get it. I have all the records to prove IRD are wrong. I will make you very stupid if this goes any further.

I never heard another word from IRD. The A'holes. They quietly buried it.

Inland Revenue B re Nugrow

After I was made redundant 1988 I was self employed for twelve years, in the end running my own company Nugrow Technologies Limited.

It was OK and I survived but as is the case of a lot of small companies who are under-capitalised, Inland Revenue got nasty.

In the end I was just not making any money, life was tough. But even though I made no money IRD said I had to pay taxes.

Life was a bitch and I had been stressed for a few years and had been keeping good records.

Eventually I was hauled in for an interview with B. I said that I am quite happy to pay my way, but that I had no money and was in debt.

She said sell your car, boat, batch etc. I said I had done most of that, she said tough.

I mentioned that I knew that the Commissioner of IRD could at his discretion wrote off taxes if it caused to much hardship or would probably not be recovered.

B said she would be a minute and go and find out. She was gone a long time and when she returned her jaw was through the floor. She said it was true but it was better if sold your boat and anyway you still had to file your tax returns.

I offered her a list of my five bank accounts and said go for it. She said how come you are being so forthcoming, I said as I had no money.

I said fine but I needed time.

The next day I wrote a letter to the District Commissioner of IRD, saying that the lady that interview me yesterday was, Ignorant, Arrogant and Divorced from Reality and I wanted an interview with a senior officer.

The battled raged for two years, they tried all sorts of tricks. They referred me to one of the big guns in a city miles away. He said I had to go and see him, I said I would if he paid the cost of the ten hour drive there and back. He also went on holiday and was supposed to assign his cases to another officer. I was trying to get in touch with him as I was really getting hassled. When he got back I gave him both barrels and he apologised.

Eventually I got my annual returns done and filed with IRD and I got an interview locally with a senior officer.

We went through the returns and she said as the amount was less than $3000 and I had no money, she would write the tax off.

She pushed several buttons on the computer and fluff they were gone. I cried at the relief of getting this big monkey off my back.

Hydraulic Jack

Now here was a character, Jack was well known and his theory was that if it was not nailed down lift it.

His feats were legendary. I would like to relate a couple of instances I was involved with.

Jack and a crew were involved in some construction work in a remote settlement. They were staying at a shearers quarters and had to provide their food and cook their own meals etc.

There was a wonderful old guy who lived there and was only too willing to share his abode. We used to play cribbage and he could look at your hand and tell you what you had in an instant.

Jack and the crew stayed for awhile, they ate all the old guys potatoes etc. packed these back in the truck and took off back to town.

I caught up with Jack and had a real go at him, (I was OIC at the time) I said how dare he abuse the hospitality of the old guy and do such a thing to him.

On another occasion I visited the crew and one of the crew was crying to me saying Jack was being very unfair. There were many kilometres from shops etc. Jack had a local friend who was supplying him with Crayfish (Lobster) and fish, Jack was taking them back to their quarters and eating them but would not share them. I had a talk to Jack and said what kind of A'hole are you, what kind of leadership was this were you are in a remote location living off the fat of the land/sea, but you will not share with your fellow workers.

In small rural communities there is plenty of wild food, pigs, deer, fish, crayfish, mussels, puha etc. It is accepted though that you share your bounty. Local Maori even having a saying, Tatou tatou, - sharing/working together.

What a Classic A'hole.

Rumour is that Jack helped himself to all and sundry while he was there as well.

Local Rastafarians

The Rastafari movement or Rasta is a monotheistic, new religious movement that arose in a Christian culture in Jamaica in the 1930s. ...
en.wikipedia.org/wiki/

We had our local version of this in the 1980s were I was working. They were a few young disaffected unemployed locals. They were heavy into the marijuana trade and smoking I guess and were particularly focused on land rights. They would say that they had land taken illegally 150 years ago. Which is partly true.

Their antics were sort of tolerated in the early days but got a bit out of hand.

One day we were working south of town and I was up on a bank. I saw the local undertaker drive past in his old fashioned hearse. (he was the local builder as well). In the back of the hearse was a coffin but also a body bag or two.

I said to the boys, oh dear looks like trouble. About an hour later the radio said there had been a local murder with someone being be-headed. It turned out it was the Rastafarians, they had been in a remote spot on a hill, and had be-headed one of their members.

Next thing we had Police all over the place, trying to find out what was happening. The locals set up virtually a vigilantly group to protect the neighbourhood.

This also was a bit of fun, because the Rastafarians fought back by threatening the ring leader of the locals the local grocery store owner. The phone call was traced and telephone people and the Police were dispatched to find were the call had come from. One person was left at the grocery store to man the phone and another technician and a Policeman went to the other end of the telephone conversation. It was at a local home.

As they approached the house S the technician yelled out there goes Diesel D (a Rastafarian) on his horse, the Policeman looked the other way and would not look at Diesel D (who could have been armed). So they did not catch their man.

Things were further heated up when the Rastafarians kidnapped one of the Detectives investigating the murder.

They then brought in the Air Force and helicopters etc.

The Police were pretty silly as they were racing round in vehicles and helicopters, the Rastafarians were racing around on horses, cutting fences and going straight to were they wanted. It was taking Police twice as long as they had to follow the road.

There was quite a bit of mayhem going on.

One night I was returning home (a distance of 40km, in the next big town), I approached Hiruharama or Jerusalem. There was about three Rastas on horse plodding along in the middle of the road. They heard me pull up behind them and eventually one of them had a little look and they parted and let me through. It was part of there intimidation of the locals, not that I was scared.

The Air Force guys would come to the Post Office Line Depot to use the telephone as they considered it more secure than the Police Station done the road.

Had a look online they are being called Ngati Dread - Maori Rastafarians, the local tribe is Ngati Porou.

From, "No Dreadlocks No Cry" the second in author Angus Gillies' series, Ngati Dread, about the Ruatoria Rastafarians, who terrorised the East Coast town from 1985 to 1990.

The Rastas had a mission to return local land to the original Ngati Porou owners and in that period more than 30 buildings were burned, including houses, a police station, a fire station, businesses, a school, churches and a marae.

The first book in the series, Footsteps of Fire, covered the philosophies and roots of the Rastas and the early crimes that cemented their fearsome reputation, such as "beating the devil out" of an acquaintance, the beheading of Lance Kupenga, the dragging of a horse which later died, and the kidnapping of a police officer.

No Dreadlocks No Cry covers most of the major fires and revisits the famous trial of five detectives for the kidnap and assault of Rasta Dick Maxwell, who claimed police had cut off his dreadlocks. It also includes a fascinating interview with Dion Hutana, the man convicted of escaping from prison,and burning down Ngati Porou Marae.

Hmm looking it up online reminds of a lot more of what happened.

Also reminds me of Big L, who later on shot a Rasta who came onto his property and was later acquitted of murder.

Crazy times.

After they quietened down they built a commune and had kids etc.

R the Drug Lord

R created a bit of local mayhem over the local drug trade. However he was also trying very hard to fleece the system.

He had several children, there was a couple with his partner in a state house no doubt getting a Government benefit and he had a couple of children at his beach home no doubt doing the same thing.

I was to OIC of the Post Office Line Depot when I got a call from R saying that his truck had a stuffed motor which had been caused by some fallen telephone wires on the way to the beach.

As this was outside my expertise I summoned a Post Office mechanic from the city to come with me to check the truck out. I said lets go round to his partners place, and sure enough R's truck was parked there. I said lets wait and see what happens. A short while later R got into the truck and headed for the beach house.

It was quite a while before he looked in the mirror and saw the Post Office truck behind him.

Needless to say he did not pursue his claim.

He thought he was bullet proof I think, this collimated in him committing a double murder over the drugs.

Big Chief T

I was involved for many years in adult education. There many ups and downs. It was quite a political atmosphere sometimes. Particularly over funding or funding cuts.

Big Chief T was in charge of the Government funding agency. She became very political and quite racist.

We fought many battles, we formed a committee to stand up for our rights. I used to be able to ring the Government Ministers Office and I was told later that Big Chief T would be crying in her office within two hours after getting a question from the Minister.

It got quite nasty and in the end a few public meetings were held to try and get rid of Big Chief T. at one meeting she said, a certain Gentleman (me) and a certain tribe (Ngati Porou) have given me grief.

At another meeting even her own people accused her of being racist to her own people.

I think in the end she resigned.

R the Magician

R was supposed to be my friend. He however was quite devious. R had big ideas and ego, but in the end it all turned to dust.

He said I was going to be a director of his big empire and that I would be heavily involved in the IT part of the business. His business plan was an inch thick (25mm), big ideas.

Later he informed me that he had decided I would just be a back room geek, I said you can forget it.

He had a bad credit rating, he asked me if he could use my credit to get a loan to buy a computer, I said fine as long as he paid the repayments.

All went fine till one day I got a phone call one day saying the payments were not being made. I contacted R and he then fluffed around. Next thing I got a visit at my office of a private detective, I would not let him in. He went and got his boss. They returned and the boss tried to get nasty. I said to him the computer was not here and you are not welcome and should leave. I asked him three times to leave as required. I then told him he was trespassing. He tried to enter the office but I bounced him off my chest, he put his fists up. I said to him go for it and you'll be up for assault.

He then rang the Police. A rookie Policeman arrived and started listening to the Private Detective. I said to the Policeman that as many acts of parliament he could I could quote as well, but the main one was that I had asked him to leave three times and he was trespassing. The Private Detective, thought about it, and then said he was satisfied the computer was not there.

I rang R about it and said no problem. I said it may not be a problem for you, but I have been visited by a Private Detective and a Policeman. And it is my credit rating that is at risk.

R arranged for the payments to be made, his attitude was very cavalier.

R did a similar thing to another friend of mine. He sold R a computer, he made some payments then just forgot about it. And yet they were both supposed to be friends.

This is all after I helped R prepare and take a case to the Employment Tribunal for his wife's unfair dismissal from a job. They got $8,000.

What an A'hole.

K the Drug King

K was a friend of mine who was a bit shady, but a nice guy.

He had a farm hidden south of the city. It was very nice and remote. No TV, no radio, but plenty of wild meat and veggies in the garden.

Even though he lost half the farm when he got divorced it was still a good place.

I spent a weekend there with K and a my girl friend we had a great time, wild mutton, potatoes from the garden, a wonderful time.

I knew K had spent some time doing the South American drug run to the USA and that he had spent some time inside in NZ as well.

I called in one day when I was passing. The door was open and I called out, no reply. I wonder around about a bit yelling out, eventually a Fijian guy showed up and said who are you what are you doing here. I said don't worry I am not the Police I am a friend of K. He said K was away. Thinking about I think the Fijian was busy planting marijuana in the forest next door.

Anyway I think it was after that I got a ring from the Police about K and a big drug bust.

He had planted a million dollars worth of marijuana in the forest and the forestry company had got pissed off with him and potted him in so to speak.

It was all in the papers. He had the farm in a family trust, but the law had been changed and his was the first family trust in NZ to be un-wound so they could take his farm under the Proceeds of Crime Act.

He got back at them by sending one of the boys down and the homestead was torched.

I spoke to K I think after he got out of jail. He said he made another silly mistake. He told his lovely Thai girlfriend were his stash was and guess what, it had disappeared and so had she.

I said to K that was a silly idea.

However K has seen the light and I have heard him twice on the radio now as a bee man an apiarist. So looks like he is going straight.

C SO

C was the boss from the city, he had a bring up that required him to visit us and give us training (I think it was annually) about the hazards we faced, especially underground and gas hazards.

I asked him several times why he only paid lip service to these things and that we had very little safety equipment to assist us and to keep us safe.

He said not to worry it did not really affect us. I said it did, we for instance potentially had gas under the hospital as it is in a geothermal area.

Anyway I got peeved off one year and thought of a way of getting back at him. We were able with out fear or favour to make suggestions to a

Suggestions Board.

So I made a suggestion that all Line Depots should have a minimum of safety gear. Hard Hats, High Visibility Jackets and Gas Detectors.

One day C arrived and opened his car and said come here and get this gear and do not do that again. I laughed and said got you!

It was in the 1970s when the boss was to be obeyed and you dare not criticise them.

Mad Bosses in R

I had several mad bosses at the place I worked for 14 years.

Mad M was a hard case, he did not seem to like me much and used to try and have a go at me.

In one instance he found us out in the country and pulled up and started yelling at me, what are you doing way out here you could have started at the other end closer to town.

I said to him I was obeying the rules as required, and had inspected the telephone line for any hazards especially power wires.

He hoped in his van and bugged off.

Another instance was when we were asked to put in an underground cable on a farmers private road. It took us a day of two. We found many years later that Mad M had been give a whole dressed (killed) mutton (sheep) as payment, yet we did all the work and saw none of it.

S the man was very impatient, and would now and then get his tits in a tangle.

The boys were once laying a cable right outside the line depot. S sat there for awhile then raced out the gate and said that they were going to slow. I do not remember exactly what he did but the up shot was they had cable everywhere and as the day was coming to end they had to cut the cable and dump it.

On another occasion he came and saw my gang working on the main road, running a cable on poles, it involved a road crossing.

S turned up and got out of his van and said you are going to slow and need to speed things up. I said we were being careful as it was a main road crossing.

S made us run miles of cable out on the ground, the idea of later putting it up on the poles. But soon after we had cars backed up on the road. Next thing J arrived with the only bus that used to run to the area.

S said that's simple, he put a wooden ladder over the cable on the road and said to the vehicles to cross it. J just shrugged his shoulders as I did. Needless to say the ladder smashed into a thousand pieces, S hopped into his van and took off, leaving us to clean up the mess.

In the middle of summer it was extremely hot and we had been working but I said to the boys (the gang was 4-5 men) we need a swim. We went back towards town but turned off down a side road and parked under a bridge on the main road were we could swim in the river.

A little later we saw S in his van racing down the road and then racing back. We sat in the river laughing our socks off.

Later at the Depot S said were the hell have you been. I said we were down a side road cutting scrub from the telephone lines. He had no option but to take our word for it.

Boss L was the worlds worst liar. He would tell so many lies he would forget which one he had used last.

The classic thing he would do would be ask me about a proposed job (I was 2IC) we may even go and look at. I would say I do not think putting the cable here is a good idea as there has been slipping in the past. I had 20+ years local knowledge.

L would the crow to the big bosses from the city that he had a brainwave and this is what we should do. I never got a mention.

The boys said why do you tell him when you know he will steal your ideas. I said I did not mind as long as it made our job easier.

H Light Fingers

H was my boy, though he was 40 years older than me.

We were working way out in the country. There was a house about 500 metres away.

After awhile H wondered off towards the house, he later returned with a big spanner. I said to him were did you find that H, he said over there in that shed, I said isn't that stealing he said no I found it in that guys shed.

He took it home, what can you do.

Once we were heading back to the depot, but H said go down to the river mouth. When we arrived we saw some guys pulling in a net that had many fish in it. H went over and talked to them (well basically he pulled rank, because of his age),. The guys loaded a sugar bag of fish in the back of our truck.

Reminds of H and food gathering. Some Fridays we would go food gathering. The great thing about a rural area is that there is tons of wild food. We went down a country road and H said s here and bring a sack. Fridays was food gathering day and H was the boss as he knew what to look for and were to go.

We went done to the creek and looked at the water cress. It looked fine to me, but H said atta its too small lets go somewhere else.

We used to get some good food and all for free.

Also reminds of our walnut episode. We used to every year go to a certain farm and get some walnuts from some large trees. We did this for many years.

However one year the farmer caught us, and complained bitterly that he sent them away to a breakfast cereal manufacturer. (I had not thought of that and had assumed they mostly went to waste).

We were sprung, but I did not have the heart to tell the farmer that we had done this for many years.

W RC D

W RC was a real hard case.

They had no idea about how to run a club especially the finances. I took over as Treasurer and was properly visited by a bailiff and presented with a bill for $3,000 from the Clubs liquor supplier. I got a shock as it is the first and last time I have been visited by a bailiff.

That season I ran the last two post match functions. We had a meeting and I showed them a spreadsheet I had done and explained the profit we made.

The first laugh was that no one opened the folder I gave them it was just passed around unopened and returned to me.

It was in the mid-80s when computers were a rare commodity.

The other laugh was that someone said, what we made a profit, we have never done that before.

I got the club (with the help of F, the secretary) back in the black.

The after match functions were sometimes hard to control, people would try and sneak in the door without paying a door charge and try and steal alcohol.

The C, D would take some alcohol home after a function, Sunday morning some coussies would come round and say, bro can we have some alcohol and we will pay you next wee. Of cause they never did pay. I had D on about it and he has hated me ever since.

The club was quite strong we even owed a section and had plans to build a clubrooms.

However after a few years some new blood took over the club. F the new Chair was going to play hell with a big stick. Got in the local paper how he was going to build a big new clubhouse etc.

After a many months of things going pretty quiet, I asked F how it was going. He was very non-committal. I asked him how the money was going and were it was going. He just said it had gone and he did not know were.

Another venture down the dunny!

A lot of ventures like this went west as the 1980 economic reforms took grip and many people left town.

It is very sad to go back now and see a lot of history in ruins.

B of the Manor

I stood for local body elections in the 1980s. I was against B of the Manor. I did not have much show beating him as he is there as of birthright.

But we wanted to get some political debate going as local body elections are very tame. It was also a time when major economic and social changes were taking place.
I rang J the editor. He said hi Bill, I said what was happening with my second article. He said verbatim, "You have had one article, that is your share of democracy". I said I can not help it if the other candidates will not debate the issue. But that was it for the Good News Times.

On the night of the Election we had a party and listened to the radio to get the results.

I lost and B of the Manor won.

We had a few more beers, someone then said, hey, why do we not go to B's place and congratulate him.

We piled into a car and went to B's place.

I knocked on the door and he was very friendly and invited us in.

B was having a silver service dinner party with friends from the city.

We sat down and had a bit of chat. We had some Maori friends with us, the white guy next to me said, are these Maoris, I never seen one of them before.

B then made a toast, verbatim, "I would like to thank the locals coming up from the village". Very quaint. Still B is nice guy and this is just his upbringing and his place in life I guess.

His house is a grand English manor.

Amazon J

This is the story of my near death experience.

I was watching TV at a friends two doors from the local hotel.

Amazon J had been drinking at the hotel. She roared off from the hotel towards my friends place. The first I heard was the roar then silence. I know that meant she was in the air.

I ran down the hill to find J strapped into her car which was on it's roof. We hauled J out and righted the car. She wanted to drive home but we said no.

F was coming from the other direction and sped to ask what was going on. I crossed the road and was talking to her. I then noticed another car leaving the hotel at speed it was L. I then realised that L was not about to s, but it was too late for me to dash across the road, so I took a deep breath and pulled my body as close as I could to F's car.

L hit the back of F's car missing me by 1 inch (25mm), it was soooo close. Luckily F's car was parked on an angle. L sped away down the road and returned to hurl abuse at F. I said man you are the drunk A'hole, you just about killed me.

The local Policeman was called and he arrived. But he was drunk too. He had been off duty.

So the whole scene was mayhem.

Mad A

A was living in a caravan at my neighbours. One night he asked W for a fork.

A short time later I was aware that something was happening two doors down, I guess it was AS, she was running down the road screaming, away from her home. AS is the estranged wife of A.

I grabbed a fence baton I kept by the bed to beat possums that came in the window.

I ran down to AS's house, I went round the back door and found it smashed to smithereens by an axe that was at the back door to cut firewood.

I looked inside and saw A sitting there quite calm.

I put the baton down and walked in talked to A. I knew by now others would have rung the Police. They arrived about an hour later to pick up A.

He was committed to a mental institution and I think he is still there.

We think what happened was that A was locked out of the caravan by a gust of wind closing the door. He wanted the fork to open the door, but that did not work.

He probably flipped then and thought oh well I will go to AS's place and stay the night there. She obviously got upset and told him to go away. A grabbed the axe and dealt to the door.

They had a small child.

You always wonder what happened to all those involved.

Online Shopping Debacle

This was extremely upsetting for me at the time, as it was a blatant money making racket based on half truths and lies.

A local accounting firm launched a world first. An online shopping mall for businesses in the city. When I saw it I was fuming as we had had a online shopping cart for city businesses for a couple of years.

Still they persisted, despite me ringing the guy in charge and yelling at him that he was an A'hole of the highest order as we had had one for years.

He just brushed me aside.

They spent thousands on advertising and for their money local businesses got a page listing their business and a description and some contact details, a very poor effort and hardly value for money.

It was a complete waste of time and a really bad experience for local business. Their web presence was just a static page, no feedback, link to products or a shopping cart.

I also contacted the local paper and spoke to the editor. I said J you remember me talking to you about our website and our shopping cart. He said oh no, I knew I should not have said a world first.

Recognition for Rosoman

But the local paper would only print this letter to the editor from my friend, and not a retraction as the accounting firm were spending thousands on advertising with the newspaper. And anyway I was a nobody.

I also found several months later that the accountant guy had rung my farmer friend M and asked about me. So they were fully aware of what they were doing.

A'holes

M DE

In 1977 one of the last manual exchanges in NZ went digital with the cut over of a NEAX exchange at R

They however also changed the way they did things.

I after the cut over was one of the faultmen. I had to wait till a telegram was sent from the big city before I could go and do a telephone fault.

This was bloody ridiculous as hell we now had modern phones and radio telephones in the trucks.

But they wanted to persevere, the subscriber had to contact the fault centre by phone. They then sent a telegram to R were I would be informed. But hell sometimes I would see subscribers in the street and they would say why have you not been around to fix my phone. I would say because I did not know about it.

After awhile I got real angry and rung M DE the big chief, whom you did not ring.

I said to him, fucking hell M this is a brothel, why do we have add layers of bureaucracy when we should be streamlining processes.

He was taken aback but he said he would think about it. It was changed shortly after.

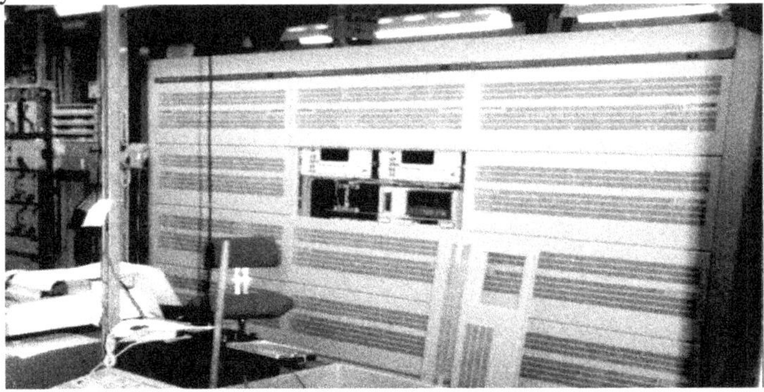

The NEAX exchange R.

Big G

G was the County Clerk.

I had brought a section of land and had to have it subdivided from a larger block of land.

The County had to approve it and then sign it off so I could get ownership of the section and build a house.

Being a bureaucratic process it took a long time.

But the most annoying thing was that the survey was all done, the papers had been filed with the County and all G had to do was sign the documents off.

I used to pass the County office twice a day on the way to work. I used to call into the County offices perhaps once a fortnight and would ask G. Have you had time to sign my documents yet and he would say no. My lawyer would write or ring G to but he just ignored us for months till he signed it.

It also reminds of a hearing we had many years prior to this, over the zoning of land in our village. They had zoned all the sections as rural so people could not build in the village. It also meant that if your house burnt down you could not rebuild. Some of the locals had owned the land for more than a thousand years.

We mounted a campaign and finally got the County to hold a hearing and look at re-zoning some of the land for building on.

We got the County Engineer to come and have a look and he said it was the Catchment Board problem, we spoke to the Catchment Board and he just laughed.

I got all the local people to file an objection to support the proposed zoning change.

The day of the hearing arrived and we all matched in and sat down. I remember one of our old people shacking at the knees. I said do not worry it is just little old C.

The hearing started, the Chairman called the hearing to order, the lawyer appearing for the Government department responsible said he would like to call the hearing to a halt, as he had not been notified that all these people would be appearing and wanting to have a say.

I said Mr Chairman I have in my hand a receipt from NZ Post saying that the proper papers were served on the department as required by the law.

The Chairman said proceed and we had the hearing.

I do not know why I had the receipt in my hand, but I knew they would try some dirty tricks.

The land was eventually rezoned to make it easier for locals to build on their sections.

Another A'hole beaten.

N got Burnt

I have a friend who's son worked in the forestry industry. The boss was a self-employed contractor with a gang of workers.

He would do things like drive two hours and then say sorry guys I forgot the keys to the gate and you will not get paid.

But the worst was that he brought new ladders etc. and took some of the money out of the guys pay. The amazing thing was that he put all the information on their time sheets.

I helped my friend prepare a case and he was taken to the Employment Tribunal by the Labour Department. We won the case but the guy just laughed as he walked out side and declared his business bankrupt.

He probably started a new business the next week, the A'hole.

What a bummer, win the case but still not to get paid.

This seems to be a common practice in the agriculture and forestry industry, even in NZ we have illegal immigrant's working in these industries, but being exploited by devious employers.

Finally

Well that is that off my chest LOL.

Still it is good to get stuff written down while you still have your marbles, I say.

I guess we should mention the biggest A'hole me!

Well I have always tried to be reasonable in life, but I decided a long time ago that you can not please all the people all the time.

I do not go out of my way to annoy people but you have to stand up for yourself in life and not let the A'holes get the better of you.

And now we have the world of the Internet. I get scammed everyday via email, telling me I have won $10 million or whatever, and at the moment

I am trying to sell my previous mobile home and get scammed all the time. I have friends that sent $1200 to some clowns in the USA, who were offering a free cruise, they even spoke to them on the phone, but a quick Google showed it was a scam. I have read of a guy paying someone for insurance etc. to some Chinese clown who wanted to buy there mobile home.

You have to ask yourself, if it is a free cruise why am I paying, if I am selling a mobile home don't they pay me not the other way round.

Jeez life is full of potholes, still I believe in human nature and you have to give life a chance!

We have just had a major earthquake in Christchurch, New Zealand and there have been mostly positive stories of people helping people. There have of cause been a few looters etc. But mostly it is a positive story of people helping neighbours and trying to do their best in a trying situation.

Some of the A'holes I have mentioned are encouraged by a business climate that allows them to get away with murder. Capitalism has a lot to answer for, when the weak and vulnerable are used and abused!

Kia Kaha and Arohanui

Other Books that may interest you

Craig Lock Books
https://www.smashwords.com/profile/view/craiglock

Ebooks
http://stores.lulu.com/craiglock

Bill Rosoman Books
http://stores.lulu.com/leftfieldnz

Ebooks
https://www.smashwords.com/profile/view/leftfieldnz

Our Main Website
http://www.creativekiwis.com

Bill Rosoman Books/Ebooks

The Ultimate Desktop Publishing Book

Desktop Publishing using Free Open Source Software.

A Brilliant Book giving You All the Tools and Examples You Need to Create That Masterpiece within You. Creating and publishing a magazine, books, posters, flyers, calendar, menu, award certificates, or business cards could Never Be Easier. Using Free Open Source Software FOSS. Scribus, Open Office, Gimp, Inkscape, Calibre. By Bill Rosoman Dip CS

http://www.lulu.com/product/paperback/the-ultimate-desktop-publishing-book/14847923

The Simple On The Road Cook Book

The Simple On The Road Cook Book. A Useful Easy, Simple and Budget Conscious Guide for Bachelors and other Food Preparation and Cooking Challenged People. Especially if Living in a Confined Space or On The Road.

http://www.lulu.com/content/paperback-book/the-simple-on-the-road-cook-book/8674457

Howto for Windows and Internet Virgins (book)

A Howto for Windows and Internet Virgins using the Windows Operating System. A Beginners Guide to using Window

http://www.lulu.com/content/paperback-book/howto-for-windows-and-internet-virgins/6121427

Te Ao Wiremu, Bill's World

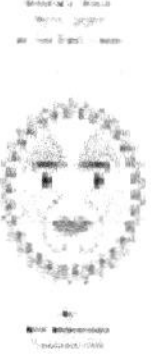

Te Ao Wiremu, Bill's World, Honorary Black, Thirty years on the East Coast. Bill Rosoman spent 29 years living and working on the East

Coast of the North Island of New Zealand above Gisborne. This is his yarn about his life there and the funny and not so funny things that happened.

http://www.lulu.com/content/paperback-book/te-ao-wiremu-bills-world/4030752

Get a Life (The Dummies Guide To Life)

The book "Get a Life (The Dummies Guide To Life)", grew out of my brushes with life and my life long study of and fascination with human nature. I also had a bout of cancer in 2006. I find it interesting how people react to big events like finding out you have cancer. Personally I believe you have to take the good with the bad and get on with it. So I decided to write my thoughts down on my laptop and see what comes up! LOL The opinions expressed are mostly my own with help from quotations etc.

http://www.lulu.com/content/paperback-book/get-a-life-%28the-dummies-guide-to-life%29/1262704
http://www.smashwords.com/books/view/31925

Android Tablet Apads How to

Android Tablets Apad How to", Some great Information for the use of Android Tablets. Tablets are the device of the future.

http://www.smashwords.com/books/view/35819

EPUB, How To Write and Publish an Ebook

An ebook, “EPUB, How To Write and Publish an Ebook”, using free software (FOSS), Writing and publishing and ebook is quite different from a hard copy book. This ebook gives you all the basic software and knowledge and skills to create your own epics for the modern age.

http://www.smashwords.com/books/view/32052

Puppy Linux Manual

An ebook, “Puppy Linux Manual”, Some great Information for the use of Puppy Linux, a Free Operating System which is great on older computers. Puppy Linux is also good for formatting and partitioning hard drives and rescuing data from crash computers.

http://www.smashwords.com/books/view/35818

Bill's Tome

An ebook, “Bill's Tome”, All That I Know Life, the Universe, Mortality etc.!

https://www.smashwords.com/books/view/41385

Creative Kiwis, an Amazing Journey

Creative Kiwis, an Amazing Journey

Bill Rosoman and Craig Lock

An ebook, "Creative Kiwis, an Amazing Journey", this book is about the journey of two people in the world of the Internet and Ebook and Book Publishing and Marketing. A massive journey and learning process.

http://www.smashwords.com/books/view/43270

A'holes That I've Known

A look at some of the A'holes I have meet in my life. Life is not always a bed of roses and you have to deal with some not so nice people. Still life is great and you move through life and it's ups and downs. Being confident, articulate and assertive is the way to go, no door mouse for me. LOL

http://www.smashwords.com/books/view/44346
http://www.lulu.com/product/paperback/aholes-that-ive-known/14963987

Craig Lock Books/Ebooks

A New Dawn

A passionate story of inspiration: hope, faith, peace and especially LOVE for the world and inspired by what I simply term God, the Creative Source of Life itself. That is my legacy to my beloved family...and the world. "But they that wait upon the Lord shall renew their strength, they shall mount up with wings as eagles; they shall run and not be weary; and they shall walk, and not faint." - Isiah 40:31

http://www.lulu.com/product/paperback/a-new-dawn/13399980
https://www.smashwords.com/books/view/42372

RETURN OF THE CHICKENS (e-book)

After that little interlude, I hope every one of you, the "New Safs" enjoy my book....and I hope you don't lynch me when you find me (like Salmon Rushdie) - something fishy going on? Because I believe that a sense of humour definitely helps in the hard but exciting years ahead of living in our "new beloved country".

http://www.lulu.com/content/e-book/return-of-the-chickens/9515900

Quote Unquote": Quotations that I like... very much (book)

This is one of my first manuscripts and a rather short one at that - just like the author. I have also included a separate section on motivational quotes for all salespeople and on business in general (see Part Two). These often helped me in my rather more formal previous commercial career. But even if you are not in business , nor in sales you might find them inspiring (or inspirational) as we journey through the game that is life. I do. ... so time to get right into it / them and get "cracking" or "weaving" as my dear mother would say.

http://www.lulu.com/content/paperback-book/quote-unquote
%e2%80%9d-quotations-that-i-like-very-much/9508150

Peace Lives Within (e-book)

These are some notes that I've made recently (from my "red book"), which is forming the basis, the frame-work, the building-blocks for a new manuscript I'm writing. So will share with you and post extracts (hopefully regularly) on my Wordpress blog (craiglock.wordpress.com) as I write it. Hopefully I'll continue getting my "daily dose of inspiration".

https://www.smashwords.com/books/view/43299
http://www.lulu.com/content/e-book/peace-lives-within/9419604

To The End Of The Rainbow (e-book)

Craig has a 'passion' for writing books that tell stories about people doing positive things in this often so hard, sometimes unkind world, occasionally so cruel, yet always amazing world He loves 'telling tales', sharing true stories that leave the reader feeling uplifted, empowered and perhaps hopefully even inspired. Craig loves to try to "test his writing limits and imagination"and is currently writing 'To The End of the Rainbow'. I don't know how my story will end, but I do know how it all began!

http://www.lulu.com/content/e-book/to-the-end-of-the-rainbow/9419597

Angolan Dawn (book)

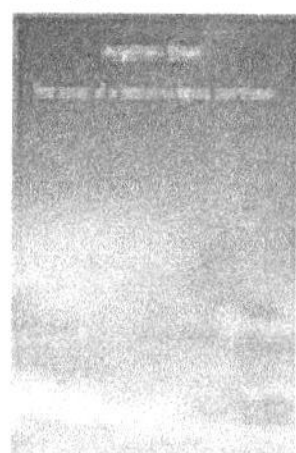

A true tale of an Angolan migrant miner who goes to 'e'Goli', the big city of gold in South Africa. Also a realistic portrayal of the Angolan conflict in "darkest Africa" through the eyes of a hospital orderly. A moving and realistic novel about the evil and destructiveness of war, as well as the inherent goodness within every human spirit. History, Angola, Southern Africa, Legacy, Gisborne, New Zealand, South Africa, Travel, Africa, War, Politics, Humanity, Conflict, Novel

http://www.lulu.com/content/paperback-book/angolan-dawn/8391177

How to Write a Book and Get Published (book)

Get Cracking and get your book written, completed and published now! We offer the complete package of helping you write that book within you and to get it published. At the end of the book you will have a published book, if you have a manuscript ready to go!

http://www.lulu.com/content/paperback-book/how-to-write-a-book-and-get-published/7313395

The New Rainbow (book)

THE NEW RAINBOW A tale of the many people in the rainbow nation of New South Africans

http://www.lulu.com/content/paperback-book/the-new-rainbow/7074514

I'LL DO IT MY WAY (book)

Childhood in South Africa, South African Politics and Apartheid and our new life in New Zealand

http://www.lulu.com/content/paperback-book/ill-do-it-my-way/6121816

Handbook for Survival in the Nineties and especially the New Millennium (book)

A collection of writings on various subjects to help every man or woman survive in a rapidly changing, uncertain world... after the "easy living and prosperity" of the seventies and eighties. An introductory look at the concepts of success, motivation, attitude, goal setting and stress

https://www.smashwords.com/books/view/43289
http://www.lulu.com/content/paperback-book/handbook-for-survival-in-the-nineties-and-especially-the-new-millenium/1660924

The End of the Line (book)

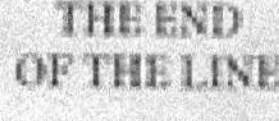

This is Craig Lock's first novel. A short novel set in "the beloved country". A passionate and heart-breaking tale of South Africa, a true story of the bad old days, but with the hope of the new. "The End Of The Line" could be described as a "faction", a fiction with a serious factual grounding. It is simple, and therefore moving. It gives yet another highly individual portrait of that troubled land, and it does so through a believable and sustained narrative form."

http://www.lulu.com/content/paperback-book/the-end-of-the-line/1630869
https://www.smashwords.com/books/view/42710

Dropped out In Godzone (book)

A new immigrant's impressions of life in provincial New Zealand (after coming from a large city in South Africa) ... and there were one or two rather funny adventures, nay escapades in "Sleepy Hollow" from time to time.

http://www.lulu.com/content/paperback-book/the-end-of-the-line/1630869
https://www.smashwords.com/books/view/42699

Over The Rainbow (book)

A look at the many colourful peoples, who make up this diverse and vibrant society, as seen through the eyes of a newspaper reporter. Many colourful "vignettes" in this "land of great contrasts" - happy, sad and true, that was the fabric of South African life in the lead up to the historic Democratic Election of 1994. We live in a very complex country of great disparities and extremes, especially in wealth and in living standards. A land of great contradictions: a land of sunshine, a world in one country, a land of laughter in this strange and beautiful place. Much of the laughter from the very people, who have suffered the most and felt the most pain in this strange tormented place of ours. Yes, there is that sadness in the eyes of them too. So to put it simply, South Africa is just one happy, sad land...and I hope that the lives of ALL South Africans will become better in the days ahead.

http://www.lulu.com/content/paperback-book/over-the-rainbow/1265824

Here There and Everywhere

Craig Lock is an extensive world traveller and failed professional emigrater who has spent most of his life's savings on airfares. He is still 'sliding down the razor blade of life', stuck on a deserted (other than a few brilliant rugby players) island at the bottom of the world near Antarctica, where he is 'trying to throw a double six' to get off and go out into the real world - but he doesn't know where! In the style of Bill Bryson, HERE, THERE AND EVERYWHERE tells tales of His hilarious hair-raising adventures in his younger years through 'Grate' Britain and the Continent.

https://www.smashwords.com/books/view/44410
http://www.lulu.com/product/paperback/here-there-and-everywhere/15050656

A'holes That I've Known

by Bill Rosoman

All Rights Reserved,
No reproduction in any form without
the permission of the Author,
Bill Rosoman, nugrownz@yahoo.com.au

First Published 2011

A look at some of the A'holes I have meet in my life. Life is not always a bed of roses and you have to deal with some not so nice people. Still life is great and you move through life and it's ups and downs. Being confident, articulate and assertive is the way to go, no door mouse for me. LOL

Keywords: Life, A'holes, Scams, Humanity, Bad People, survival, humour, humor, ripoffs, confident, articulate, assertive

###